A 90-Day Walk with God

A Journey to Renewal, Restoration, and Revival

John K. Lomax

Copyright © [2025] John K. Lomax

Dedication

To My Wife Dorothy for her sustaining love, to my sons Felix and Faithy, my granddaughter Daijah.and to all my siblings Carson, Mary, Wilhelmina, and Janice and their amazing families! Love you all!

Acknowledgments

Thanks Be To Almighty God and my Savior Jesus Christ for His Tender Mercies and Abounding Grace.

Contents

Introduction 1
Why I wrote this guide? 2
Making The Most of This Guide 5
Week 1: A New Beginning 8
   Daily Entries: 8
Week 2: Trusting God Completely 15
   Daily Entries: 15
Week 3: The Power of Forgiveness 22
   Daily Entries: 22
Week 4: Your Identity in Christ 29
   Daily Entries: 29
Week 5: Walking in Faith 36
   Daily Entries: 36
Week 6: The Joy of the Lord 43
   Daily Entries: 43
Week 7: Navigating Life's Challenges 50
   Daily Entries: 50
Week 8: Discovering Your Purpose 57
   Daily Entries: 57
Week 9: Deepening Prayer & Meditation 64
   Daily Entries: 64
Week 10: Serving Others 71
   Daily Entries: 71

Week 11: Overcoming Spiritual Dryness 78
   Daily Entries: 78
Week 12: Living a Transformed Life 85
   Daily Entries: 85
Week 13: A Thankful Heart 92
   Daily Entries: 92
Final Thoughts 98

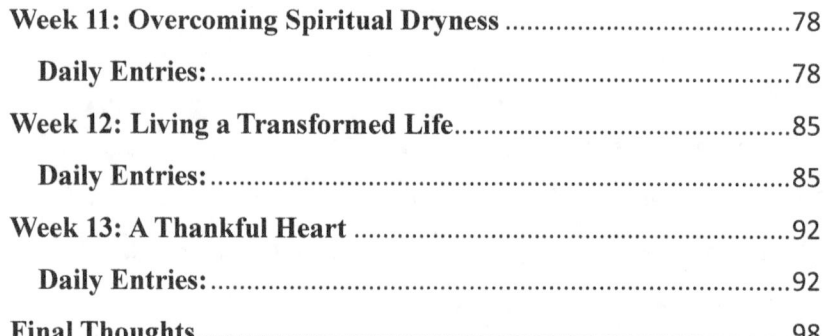

Introduction

Welcome to your **90-day walk with God**—a journey of renewal, restoration, and revival. Whether you feel spiritually distant, seek deeper faith, or want to strengthen your relationship with God, this guide will help you grow. Each week has a theme with a foundational scripture, daily supporting scriptures, short prayers, and reflection days to help you meditate on God's Word.

Why I wrote this guide?

Recently, while doing my personal mediation, I was listening to Tamela Mann's gospel hit "Take Me to the King". That day, it stirred something deep within me. As I listened to the words:

Truth is I'm tired, options are few. I'm trying to pray, but where are You?

I'm all churched out, hurt and abused. I can't fake, what's left to do?

I thought about the countless people—both inside and outside the church—who feel **exactly like this**. Spiritually drained. Weary. Disconnected from God. Some have been faithful believers for years but now feel **stuck in a season of apathy**. Others are searching for something deeper, but their past or present struggles **leave them feeling unworthy**.

As I meditated on these words, it was as if the **Spirit of the Lord** spoke to me, asking:

"Do you know how many people feel this way? How many people go through different seasons in their faith? How often do believers need to be restored, revitalized, and re-energized?"

That moment inspired me to write this guide. I realized that so many believers experience different seasons in their faith journey—some moments of great strength, and others where they feel lost, exhausted, and in need of spiritual revival. It reminded me why this guide is so important: to provide a structured path for renewal, to help people draw closer to God, and to encourage those who feel distant or weary to take a step back toward Him.

This guide is for anyone who feels:

✓ **Tired and spiritually exhausted**

✓ **Disconnected from God and searching for renewal**

✓ **Like their faith has faded, but they long to get back to Him**

✓ **Like they need healing from past hurts, disappointments, or failures**

✓ **Eager to grow in their faith but unsure where to start**

✓ **Anyone who simply wants to be revived and deepen their walk with God**

I wanted this to be more than just **a devotional**—I wanted it to be **a journey**. A journey of **renewal, restoration, and revival** that walks you through **scripture, reflection, and prayer** over 90 days. My prayer is that by the end of this guide, you will **experience God's presence in a fresh way, feel spiritually revived, and know beyond a doubt that He is still working in your life.**

It was also important for me that people be able to complete this meditation in **10 to 15 minutes a day**. People's lives are so busy that I wanted to take away any excuses for not doing daily meditation. This guide is structured so that no matter how hectic your day may be, you can still find time to connect with God and reflect on His word.

If you've ever felt like you don't have much to bring, if your heart has ever felt **torn in pieces**, this is your **offering to God**—your surrender, your willingness to take one step at a time.

I believe your breakthrough is coming.

Let's walk this journey together.

To God Be The Glory.

John K. Lomax

Making The Most of This Guide

To fully experience the renewal and transformation God has for you, I encourage you to commit to this journey daily. Each day includes a guiding thought, a scripture for meditation, a short prayer, and space for reflection. Here are a few ways to maximize your experience:

1 **Set aside time each day** – Whether morning or evening, create a sacred space to engage with God.

2 **Journal your reflections** – Writing your thoughts and prayers will help deepen your connection with the material.

3 **Pray intentionally** – Ask God to reveal His truth and speak to your heart each day.

4 **Apply what you learn** – Take small, intentional steps to live out your renewed faith.

5 **Consider sharing your journey** – If possible, walk through this guide with a friend or group for encouragement and accountability.

6 **Have a Bible with you** – I recommend that you have a **Bible** where you can open and study each day. It can be a **physical book or a digital device**, but you need the **Word of God in your hand** to truly engage in the journey.

7 **Use this guide in a study group** – If you are in a **weekly study group, like a Bible study that meets once a week**, study the **previous week's readings before you meet** and jot down your journal thoughts. This will help you bring insights to your discussion. You can complete this weekly

discussion **in-person** (which is the best option) or **virtually over Zoom or Teams**. A **weekly group session** should take about **one hour to an hour and a half** to go over key themes, share experiences, and encourage one another.

This is more than just a book—it's a life-changing journey. I believe that by the end of these 90 days, you will experience renewal, restoration, and revival in your walk with God. May He bless your journey abundantly!

How the Devotional Is Structured

- Each day includes:
  - A **Guiding Thought** related to the weekly theme.
  - A **Scripture** passage for meditation.
  - A **Short Prayer** to center your heart.
  - **Journaling Space** for personal reflection.
- **Reflection Days** encourage deeper engagement.
- **Summary Days** allow you to review what you've learned.
- **Day 90** is a special day to write a thank-you note to God.

Now, let's begin this **90-day walk with God!**

Week 1: A New Beginning

Theme Scripture: *2 Corinthians 5:17* – "Therefore, if anyone is in Christ, the new creation has come: The old has gone, the new is here!"

Daily Entries:

Day 1: *God's Mercies Are New Every Morning*
Scripture: Lamentations 3:22-23

Prayer: Lord, thank You for Your endless mercies. Help me embrace this new beginning with faith. Amen.

Journal Reflection: How does knowing that God gives you a fresh start each day change your perspective?

Journal Entry:

_____

_____

_____

_____

_____

_____

_____

Day 2: *God is Doing a New Thing*
Scripture: Isaiah 43:19

Prayer: Father, open my eyes to the new things You are doing in my life. Help me trust Your plan. Amen.

Journal Reflection: Where in your life do you need God's renewal?

Journal Entry:

Day 3: *Walking in Newness of Life*
Scripture: Romans 6:4

Prayer: Jesus, as I walk with You, may I live out the new life You have given me. Amen.

Journal Reflection: What old habits do you need to leave behind?

Journal Entry:

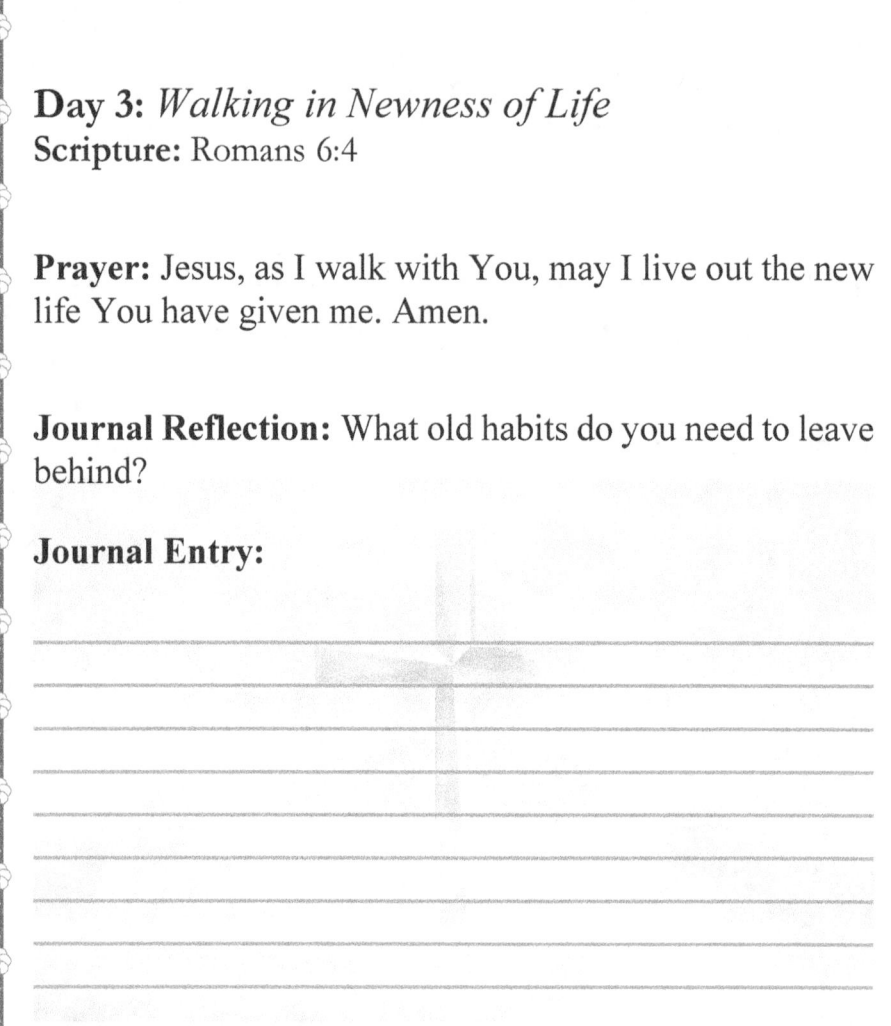

Day 4: *A New Heart and Spirit*
Scripture: Ezekiel 36:26

Prayer: Lord, renew my heart and spirit so that I may live fully in Your love. Amen.

Journal Reflection: What areas of your heart need transformation?

Journal Entry:

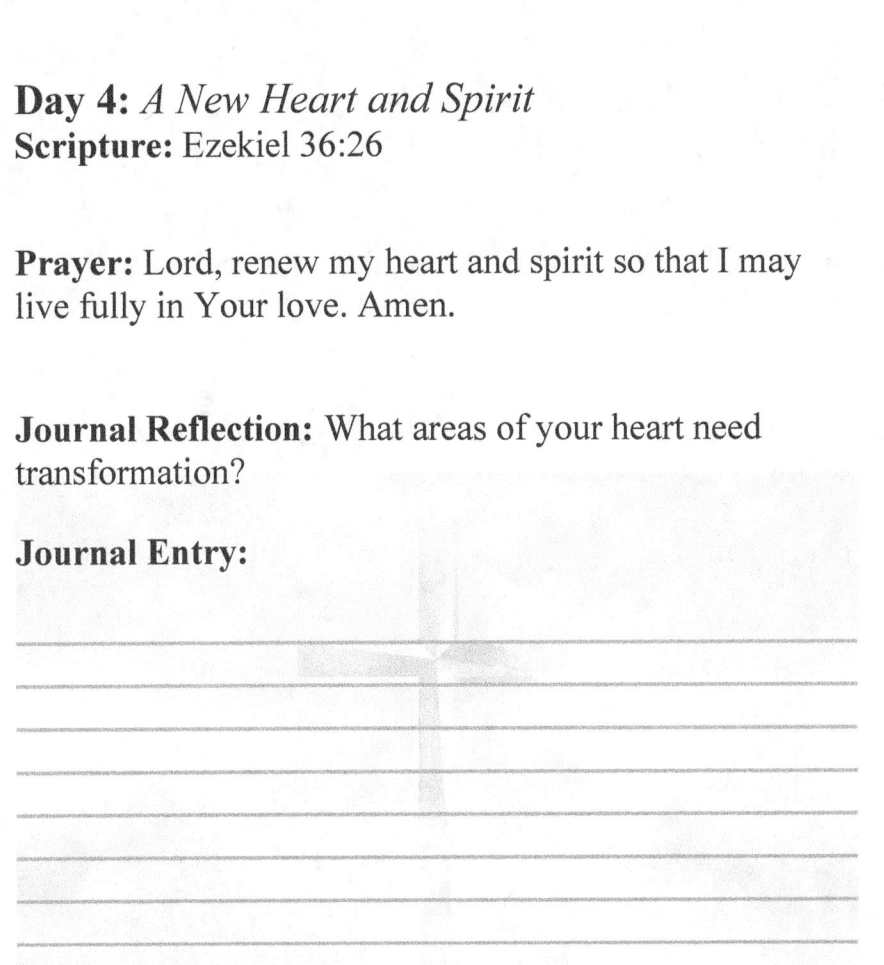

Day 5: *God Finishes What He Starts*
Scripture: Philippians 1:6

Prayer: Father, I trust that You will complete the good work You have started in me. Amen.

Journal Reflection: What is one way you see God working in your life?

Journal Entry:

Day 6: Reflection Day:

Spend time journaling about what God is teaching you this week about a new beginning.

Journal Entry:

Day 7: Summary Day

Review the week's scriptures and journal any final thoughts about starting anew.

Journal Entry:

This completes **Week 1: A New Beginning**. Now let's begin **Week 2: Trusting God Completely.**

Week 2: Trusting God Completely

Theme Scripture: *Proverbs 3:5-6* – "Trust in the LORD with all your heart and lean not on your own understanding; in all your ways submit to him, and he will make your paths straight."

Daily Entries:

Day 8: *Trust Over Fear*
Scripture: Psalm 56:3

Prayer: Lord, help me choose trust over fear in every situation. Amen.

Journal Reflection: Where do you struggle to trust God?

Journal Entry:

_____
_____
_____
_____
_____
_____
_____
_____

Day 9: *Perfect Peace Comes from Trust*
Scripture: Isaiah 26:3-4

Prayer: Father, may my heart remain steadfast in You, knowing that perfect peace comes from trusting You. Amen.

Journal Reflection: What areas of your life need God's peace?

Journal Entry:

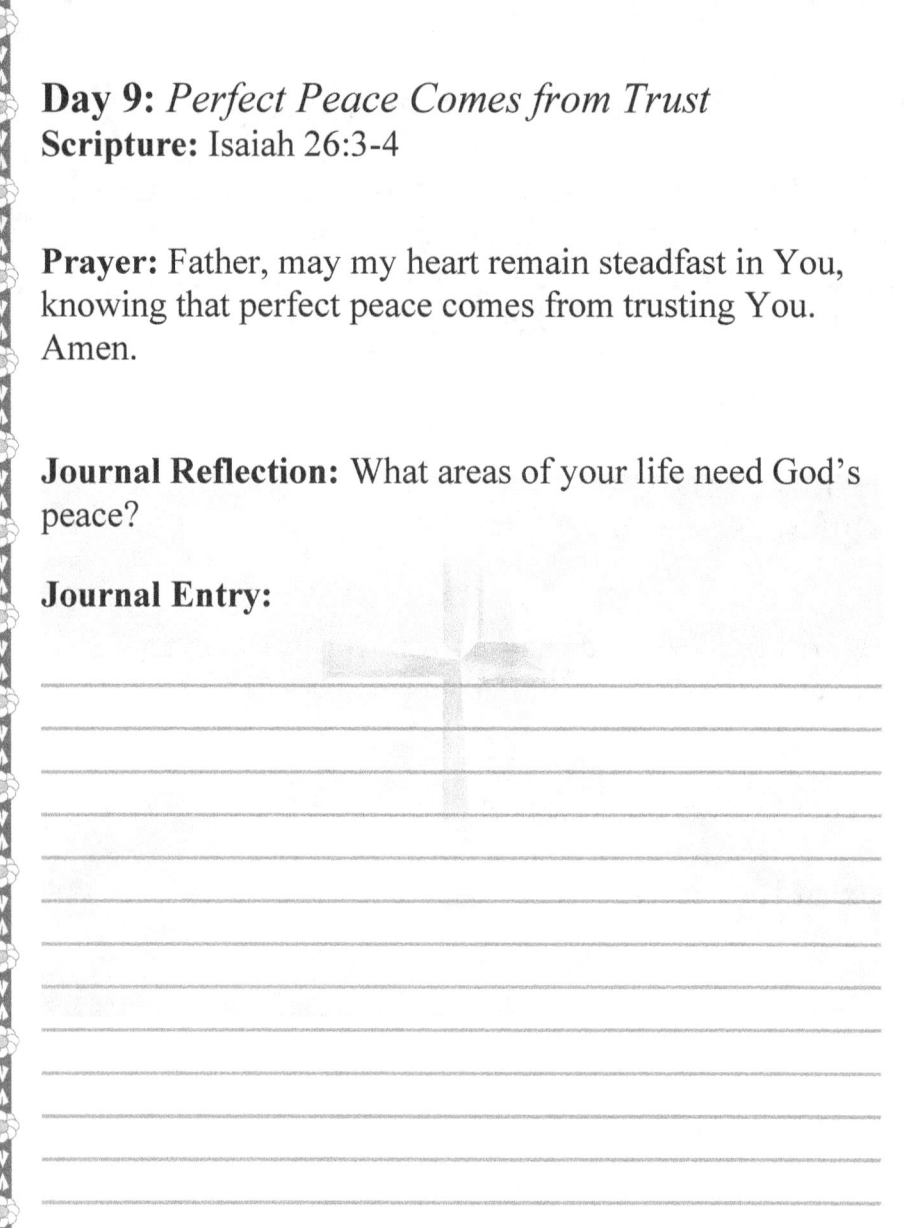

Day 10: *Do Not Worry, God Provides*
Scripture: Matthew 6:25-27

Prayer: Lord, help me release my worries and trust in Your faithful provision. Amen.

Journal Reflection: What worries do you need to surrender to God today?

Journal Entry:

Day 11: *God's Plans are for Good*
Scripture: Jeremiah 29:11

Prayer: Lord, thank You for having a plan for my life, a future full of hope and purpose. Amen.

Journal Reflection: How does trusting in God's plans bring you peace?

Journal Entry:

Day 12: *God Has Not Given Us a Spirit of Fear*
Scripture: 2 Timothy 1:7

Prayer: Father, remove all fear from my heart and fill me with Your power, love, and self-discipline. Amen.

Journal Reflection: How can you walk in bold faith today?

Journal Entry:

Day 13: Reflection Day

Spend time journaling about what God is teaching you this week about trusting him completely.

Journal Entry:

Day 14: Summary Day

Review the week's scriptures and journal any final thoughts on trusting God completely.

Journal Entry:

_____
_____
_____
_____
_____
_____
_____
_____
_____
_____
_____
_____
_____
_____
_____
_____

This completes **Week 2: Trusting God Completely**. Now Let Us Begin **Week 3: The Power of Forgiveness**.

Week 3: The Power of Forgiveness

Theme Scripture: *Ephesians 4:32* – "Be kind and compassionate to one another, forgiving each other, just as in Christ God forgave you."

Daily Entries:

Day 15: *The Call to Forgive*
Scripture: Matthew 6:14-15

Prayer: Lord, help me to forgive as You have forgiven me. Teach me to release all bitterness and embrace Your peace. Amen.

Journal Reflection: In what area of your life do you struggle to forgive?

Journal Entry:

_____
_____
_____
_____
_____
_____
_____

Day 16: *Judging Others with Mercy*
Scripture: Luke 6:37

Prayer: Father, help me to show mercy instead of judgment. May I extend grace to others as You have done for me. Amen.

Journal Reflection: How can showing mercy change your perspective on someone who has hurt you?

Journal Entry:

_____
_____
_____
_____
_____
_____
_____
_____
_____
_____
_____

Day 17: *Forgiving as Christ Forgave*
Scripture: Colossians 3:13

Prayer: Jesus, Your forgiveness is my example. Help me to let go of past hurts and walk in freedom. Amen.

Journal Reflection: What does it mean to forgive as Christ forgave you?

Journal Entry:

Day 18: *God Removes Our Sins*
Scripture: Psalm 103:12

Prayer: Lord, thank You for removing my sins as far as the east is from the west. Help me to forgive myself and others. Amen.

Journal Reflection: How does knowing that God completely removes your sins impact your ability to forgive?

Journal Entry:

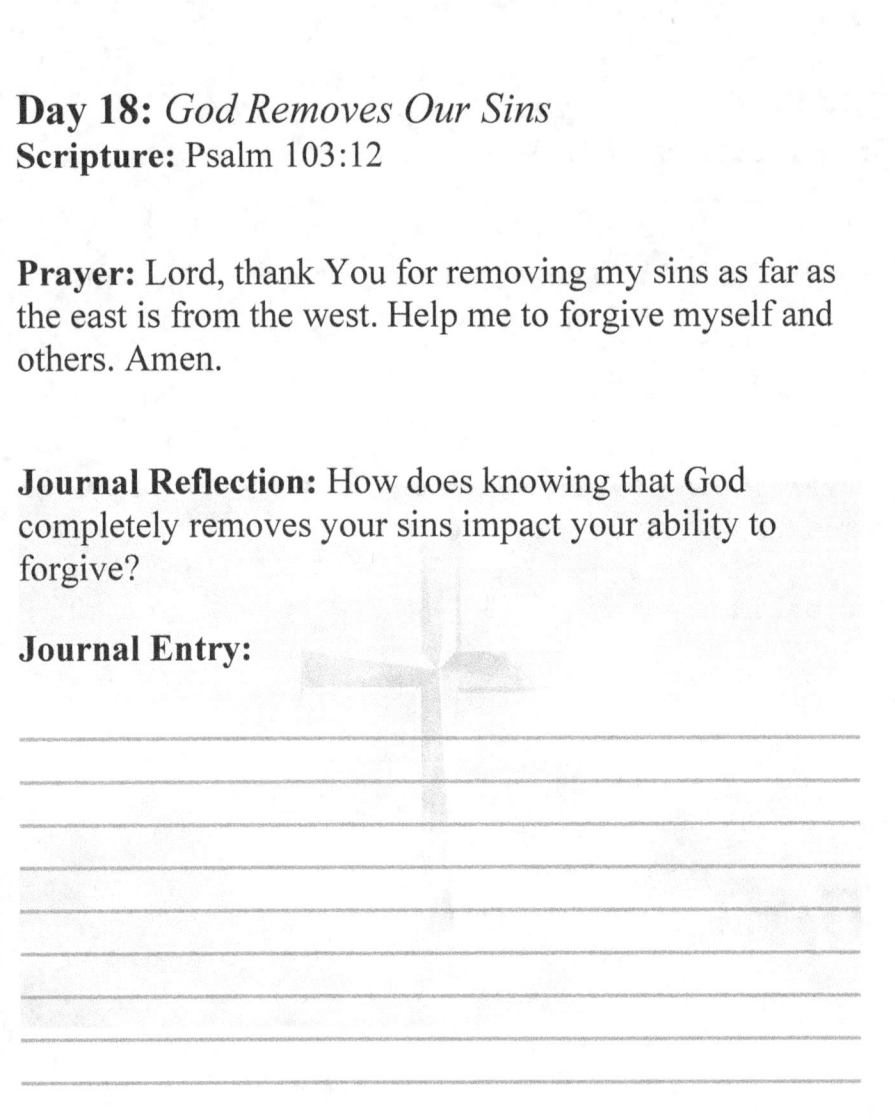

Day 19: *God's Compassion in Forgiveness*
Scripture: Micah 7:18-19

Prayer: Father, You delight in showing mercy. Help me to reflect that same compassion in my relationships. Amen.

Journal Reflection: How does God's mercy toward you inspire you to show mercy to others?

Journal Entry:

Day 20: Reflection Day

Spend time journaling about what God is teaching you this week about the power of forgiveness.

Journal Entry:

Day 21: Summary Day
Review the week's scriptures and journal any final thoughts on the power of forgiveness.

Journal Entry:

This completes **Week 3: The Power of Forgiveness**. Let us move on to **Week 4: Your Identity In Christ**

Week 4: Your Identity in Christ

Theme Scripture: *Galatians 2:20* – "I have been crucified with Christ, and I no longer live, but Christ lives in me."

Daily Entries:

Day 22: *You Are a New Creation*
Scripture: 2 Corinthians 5:17

Prayer: Lord, help me to see myself as You see me—a new creation in Christ. Amen.

Journal Reflection: How does knowing you are a new creation impact your life?

Journal Entry:

Day 23: *Chosen and Adopted by God*
Scripture: Ephesians 1:4-5

Prayer: Father, thank You for choosing me and adopting me as Your child. Amen.

Journal Reflection: What does being chosen by God mean to you?

Journal Entry:

Day 24: *A Royal Priesthood, A Holy Nation*
Scripture: 1 Peter 2:9

Prayer: Lord, help me to embrace my identity as part of Your royal priesthood and holy nation. Amen.

Journal Reflection: How does knowing you are set apart for God change the way you live?

Journal Entry:

Day 25: *A Child of God*
Scripture: Romans 8:16-17

Prayer: Father, thank You for making me Your child and an heir to Your kingdom. Amen.

Journal Reflection: What does it mean to you to be a child of God?

Journal Entry:

Day 26: *Fearfully and Wonderfully Made*
Scripture: Psalm 139:13-14

Prayer: Lord, help me to see myself as You have created me—fearfully and wonderfully made. Amen.

Journal Reflection: How does embracing your God-given identity impact your confidence and faith?

Journal Entry:

Day 27: Reflection Day

Spend time journaling about what God is teaching you this week about your identity in Christ.

Journal Entry:

Day 28: Summary Day

Review the week's scriptures and journal any final thoughts on what God is teaching you about your identity in Christ.

Journal Entry:

_____
_____
_____
_____
_____
_____
_____
_____
_____
_____
_____
_____

This completes **Week 4: Your Identity in Christ**. Now let's get ready for **Week 5: Walking In Faith.**

Week 5: Walking in Faith

Theme Scripture: *Hebrews 11:1* – "Now faith is confidence in what we hope for and assurance about what we do not see."

Daily Entries:

Day 29: *Walking by Faith, Not by Sight*
Scripture: 2 Corinthians 5:7

Prayer: Lord, help me to trust You completely, even when I cannot see the full picture. Amen.

Journal Reflection: How can you practice walking by faith today?

Journal Entry:

Day 30: *Doubt vs. Faith*
Scripture: James 1:6

Prayer: Father, strengthen my faith so that I do not waver in doubt but trust fully in You. Amen.

Journal Reflection: What doubts are you holding onto that you need to surrender to God?

Journal Entry:

Day 31: *Faith and Action*
Scripture: James 2:17

Prayer: Lord, let my faith be alive and active, demonstrated by my actions. Amen.

Journal Reflection: How can you live out your faith through action today?

Journal Entry:

Day 32: *Faith the Size of a Mustard Seed*
Scripture: Matthew 17:20

Prayer: Father, increase my faith so that I trust in You even for the impossible. Amen.

Journal Reflection: What is something big that you need to trust God for?

Journal Entry:

Day 33: *Strengthened by Faith*
Scripture: Romans 4:20-21

Prayer: Lord, help me to be unwavering in my faith, trusting Your promises completely. Amen.

Journal Reflection: How can you strengthen your faith today?

Journal Entry:

Day 34: Reflection Day
Spend time journaling about what God is teaching you this week about walking in faith.

Journal Entry:

Day 35: Summary Day

Review the week's scriptures and journal any final thoughts about walking in faith.

Journal Entry:

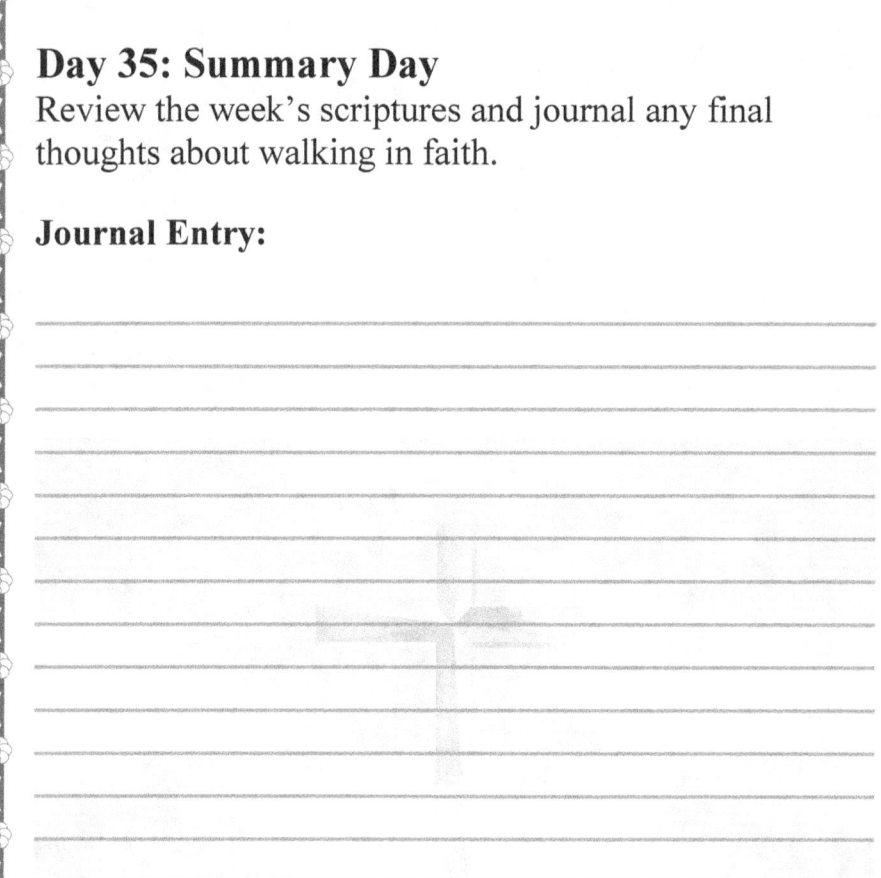

This completes **Week 5: Walking in Faith**. Next, we will study in **Week 6: The Joy of The Lord**

Week 6: The Joy of the Lord

Theme Scripture: *Nehemiah 8:10* – "The joy of the Lord is your strength."

Daily Entries:

Day 36: *Finding Joy in God's Presence*
Scripture: Psalm 16:11

Prayer: Lord, help me to find the fullness of joy in Your presence. Amen.

Journal Reflection: How does being in God's presence bring you joy?

Journal Entry:

_____
_____
_____
_____
_____
_____
_____
_____
_____

Day 37: *Rejoice in the Lord Always*
Scripture: Philippians 4:4

Prayer: Father, teach me to rejoice in You no matter what my circumstances are. Amen.

Journal Reflection: What are some things you can rejoice about today?

Journal Entry:

Day 38: *Joy in Salvation*
Scripture: Isaiah 12:3

Prayer: Lord, let me draw joyfully from the well of salvation each day. Amen.

Journal Reflection: How does your salvation bring joy to your life?

Journal Entry:

Day 39: *Joy That Remains*
Scripture: John 15:11

Prayer: Jesus, fill me with the joy that comes from abiding in You. Amen.

Journal Reflection: How can you remain in Christ and experience lasting joy?

Journal Entry:

Day 40: *The Fruit of Joy*
Scripture: Galatians 5:22-23

Prayer: Holy Spirit, develop the fruit of joy in my life so that I may reflect Your goodness. Amen.

Journal Reflection: How can you cultivate joy as part of your daily walk with God?

Journal Entry:

Day 41: Reflection Day

Spend time journaling about what God is teaching you this week about living in His joy.

Journal Entry:

Day 42: Summary Day

Review the week's scriptures and journal any final thoughts on walking and living in the joy of the Lord.

Journal Entry:

_____
_____
_____
_____
_____
_____
_____
_____
_____
_____
_____
_____
_____
_____

This completes **Week 6: The Joy of the Lord**. Now let's explore **Week 7: Navigating Life's Challenges**

Week 7: Navigating Life's Challenges

Theme Scripture: *John 16:33* – "In this world you will have trouble. But take heart! I have overcome the world."

Daily Entries:

Day 43: *God is Our Refuge in Trouble*
Scripture: Psalm 46:1

Prayer: Lord, remind me that You are my refuge and strength in every trial. Amen.

Journal Reflection: How can you rely on God in the face of difficulty?

Journal Entry:

Day 44: *Peace in the Midst of the Storm*
Scripture: Philippians 4:6-7

Prayer: Father, help me not to be anxious but to rest in Your peace. Amen.

Journal Reflection: What worries do you need to surrender to God today?

Journal Entry:

Day 45: *God's Strength in Our Weakness*
Scripture: 2 Corinthians 12:9

Prayer: Jesus, let Your grace be my strength in times of weakness. Amen.

Journal Reflection: How can God's grace sustain you in difficult moments?

Journal Entry:

Day 46: *Do Not Fear, God is With You*
Scripture: Isaiah 41:10

Prayer: Lord, help me trust that You are with me in every trial. Amen.

Journal Reflection: How does knowing God is with you bring comfort?

Journal Entry:

Day 47: *Overcoming Through Faith*
Scripture: 1 John 5:4

Prayer: Father, strengthen my faith so that I may overcome life's challenges. Amen.

Journal Reflection: How can faith help you persevere through hardships?

Journal Entry:

Day 48: Reflection Day

Spend time journaling about what God is teaching you this week about navigating life's challenges.

Journal Entry:

Day 49: Summary Day

Review the week's scriptures and journal any final thoughts on navigating life's challenges.

Journal Entry:

This completes **Week 7: Navigating Life's Challenges**. Let's move forward into **Week 8: Discovering Your Purpose!**

Week 8: Discovering Your Purpose

Theme Scripture: *Jeremiah 29:11* – "For I know the plans I have for you, declares the Lord, plans to prosper you and not to harm you, plans to give you hope and a future."

Daily Entries:

Day 50: *God's Plan for You*
Scripture: Proverbs 19:21

Prayer: Lord, help me trust that Your purpose for my life is greater than my own plans. Amen.

Journal Reflection: How can you align your plans with God's purpose?

Journal Entry:

_____
_____
_____
_____
_____
_____
_____

Day 51: *Created for Good Works*
Scripture: Ephesians 2:10

Prayer: Father, thank You for preparing good works for me to walk in. Show me how to fulfill my purpose. Amen.

Journal Reflection: What are some ways you can serve God with the gifts He has given you?

Journal Entry:

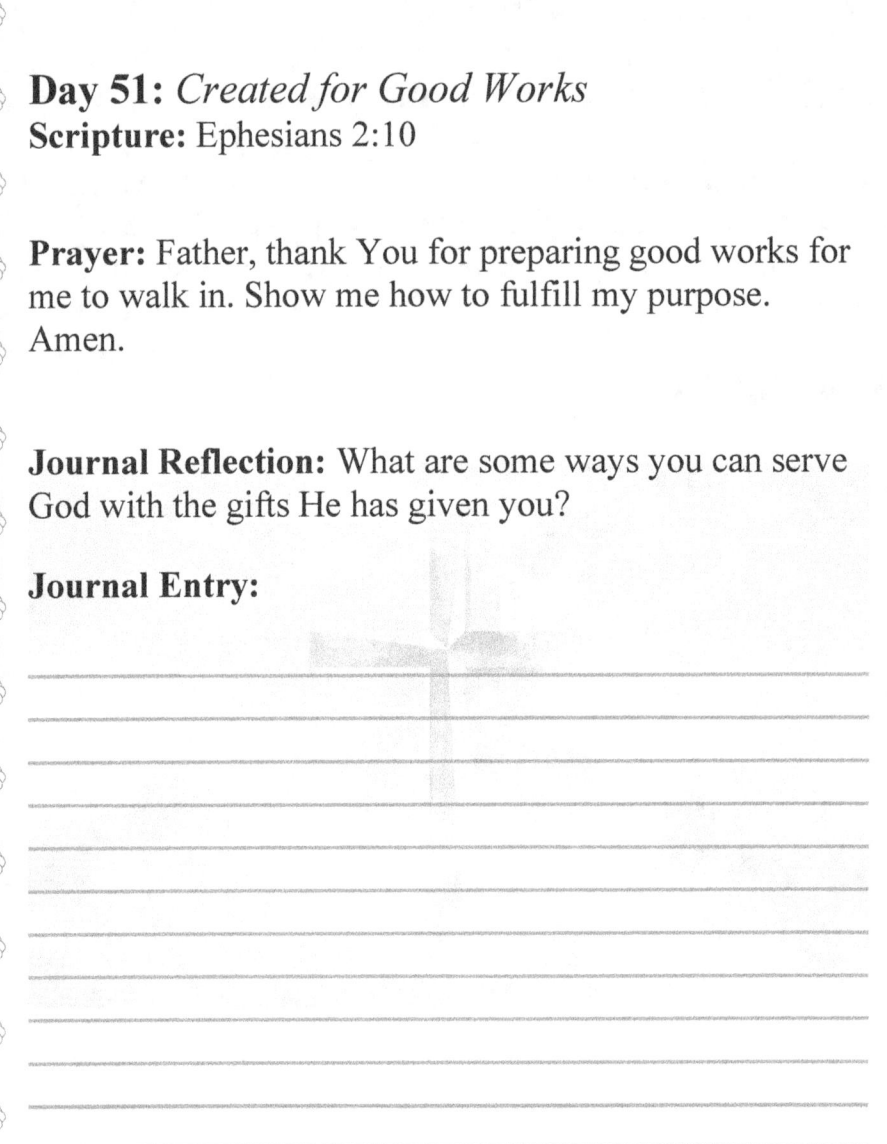

Day 52: *Seeking God's Guidance*
Scripture: Psalm 32:8

Prayer: Lord, lead me in the way I should go and give me wisdom to follow Your path. Amen.

Journal Reflection: How do you seek God's guidance when making decisions?

Journal Entry:

Day 53: *Walking in Your Calling*
Scripture: 2 Timothy 1:9

Prayer: Jesus, help me embrace the calling You have placed on my life with confidence and obedience. Amen.

Journal Reflection: What steps can you take to walk in your God-given calling?

Journal Entry:

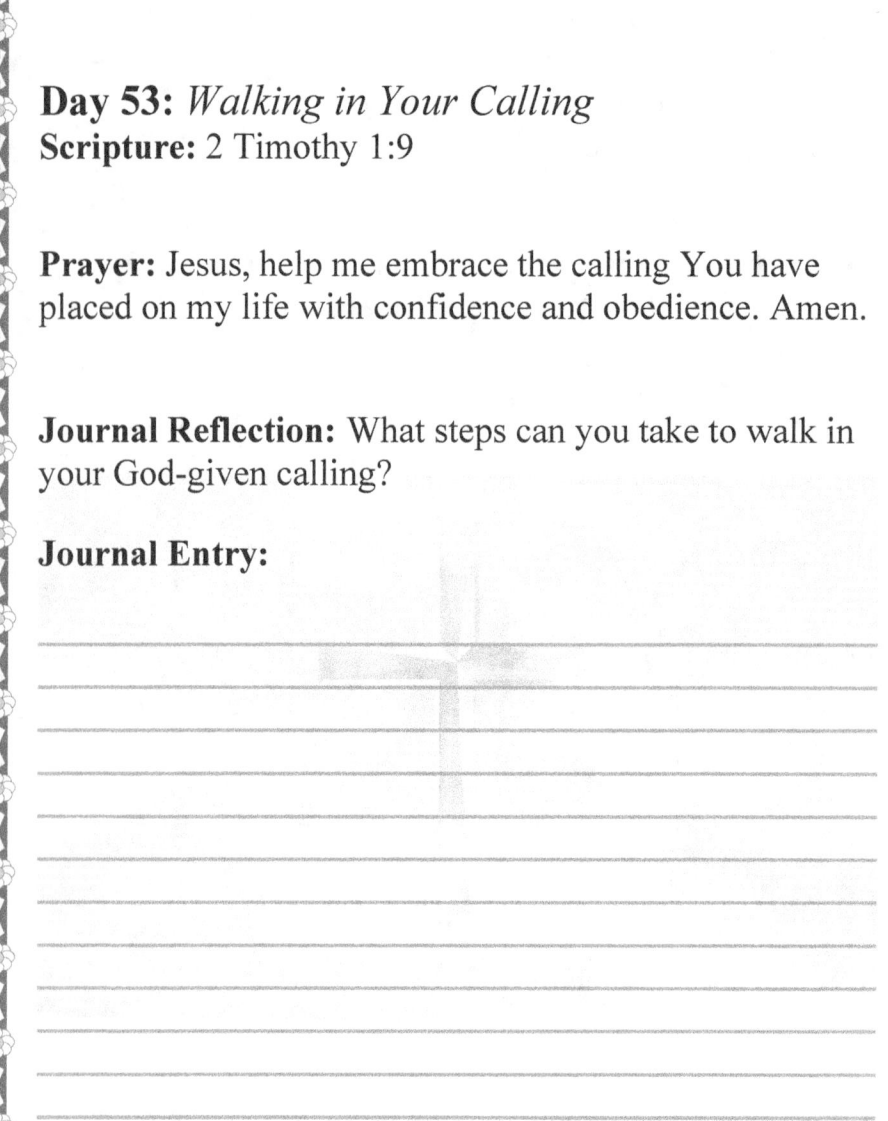

Day 54: *Glorifying God in All You Do*
Scripture: Colossians 3:23-24

Prayer: Lord, help me to work with excellence and joy, knowing that I serve You in all things. Amen.

Journal Reflection: How can you glorify God in your work and daily tasks?

Journal Entry:

Day 55: Reflection Day

Spend time journaling about what God is teaching you this week on discovering your purpose.

Journal Entry:

Day 56: Summary Day

Review the week's scriptures and journal any final thoughts on discovering your purpose.

Journal Entry:

This completes **Week 8: Discovering Your Purpose**. Let's move on to **Week 9: Deepening Prayer and Meditation**

Week 9: Deepening Prayer & Meditation

Theme Scripture: *Philippians 4:6-7* – "Do not be anxious about anything, but in every situation, by prayer and petition, with thanksgiving, present your requests to God. And the peace of God, which transcends all understanding, will guard your hearts and your minds in Christ Jesus."

Daily Entries:

Day 57: *The Power of Prayer*
Scripture: 1 Thessalonians 5:16-18

Prayer: Lord, help me develop a heart that seeks You in prayer every day. Amen.

Journal Reflection: How can you make prayer a greater priority in your life?

Journal Entry:

_____
_____
_____
_____
_____
_____

Day 58: *Praying with Confidence*
Scripture: Hebrews 4:16

Prayer: Father, let me boldly come before You, knowing that You hear my prayers. Amen.

Journal Reflection: How does knowing God hears your prayers change how you approach Him?

Journal Entry:

Day 59: *Meditating on God's Word*
Scripture: Joshua 1:8

Prayer: Lord, teach me to meditate on Your Word day and night so that I may live according to Your will. Amen.

Journal Reflection: How can you incorporate more scripture meditation into your daily routine?

Journal Entry:

Day 60: *Seeking God's Presence in Silence*
Scripture: Psalm 46:10

Prayer: Help me to be still and recognize Your presence, Lord. Amen.

Journal Reflection: When was the last time you sat in silence before God?

Journal Entry:

Day 61: *Thanksgiving in Prayer*
Scripture: Colossians 4:2

Prayer: Lord, help me to develop a thankful heart that finds joy in every situation. Amen.

Journal Reflection: What are three things you are grateful for today?

Journal Entry:

Day 62: Reflection Day

Spend time journaling about what God is teaching you this week about studying His Word, prayer, and meditation.

Journal Entry:

Day 63: Summary Day

Review the week's scriptures and journal any final thoughts on deepening prayer and meditating on God's Word.

Journal Entry:

This completes **Week 9: Deepening Prayer and Meditation** now we turn our attention to **Week 10: Serving Others**

Week 10: Serving Others

Theme Scripture: *Mark 10:45* – "For even the Son of Man did not come to be served, but to serve, and to give his life as a ransom for many."

Daily Entries:

Day 64: *The Heart of a Servant*
Scripture: Matthew 23:11

Prayer: Jesus, help me develop a heart that joyfully serves others as You did. Amen.

Journal Reflection: How can you serve someone today?

Journal Entry:

_____
_____
_____
_____
_____
_____
_____
_____

Day 65: *Serving in Humility*
Scripture: Philippians 2:3-4

Prayer: Lord, teach me to serve with humility and put others before myself. Amen.

Journal Reflection: Why is humility important when serving others?

Journal Entry:

Day 66: *Loving Through Service*
Scripture: Galatians 5:13

Prayer: Help me use my freedom in Christ to love and serve others. Amen.

Journal Reflection: How does serving others demonstrate God's love?

Journal Entry:

Day 67: *Serving Without Expecting Anything in Return*
Scripture: Luke 6:35

Prayer: Lord, let me serve with a heart that seeks no reward but glorifies You. Amen.

Journal Reflection: How can you serve others selflessly this week?

Journal Entry:

Day 68: *God Rewards Faithful Service*
Scripture: Colossians 3:23-24

Prayer: Help me to work heartily as if I am serving You, Lord. Amen.

Journal Reflection: How does knowing that God sees your service encourage you?

Journal Entry:

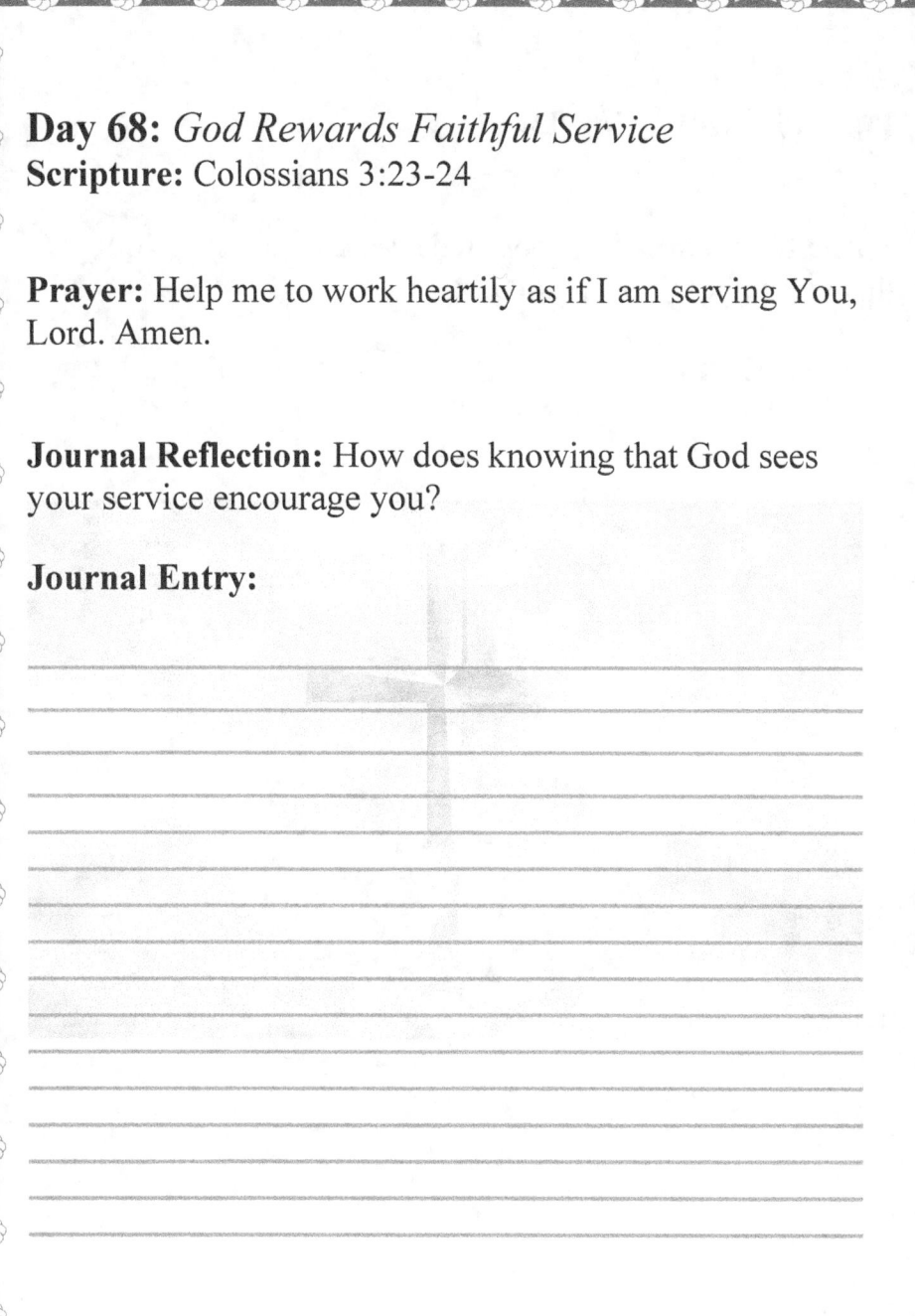

Day 69: Reflection Day

Spend time journaling about what God is teaching you this week about serving others.

Journal Entry:

Day 70: Summary Day

Review the week's scriptures and journal any final thoughts on serving others.

Journal Entry:

_____
_____
_____
_____
_____
_____
_____
_____
_____
_____
_____
_____
_____
_____
_____

This completes **Week 10: Serving Others**. Let's now focus on **Week 11: Overcoming Spiritual Dryness**

Week 11: Overcoming Spiritual Dryness

Theme Scripture: *Psalm 42:1-2* – "As the deer pants for streams of water, so my soul pants for you, my God. My soul thirsts for God, for the living God."

Daily Entries:

Day 71: *Seeking God in Dry Seasons*
Scripture: Isaiah 58:11

Prayer: Lord, guide me and refresh my soul during times of spiritual dryness. Amen.

Journal Reflection: How can you seek God more earnestly during dry seasons?

Journal Entry:

_____
_____
_____
_____
_____
_____
_____

Day 72: *Resting in God's Presence*
Scripture: Matthew 11:28-30

Prayer: Jesus, I come to You for rest and renewal. Strengthen my spirit. Amen.

Journal Reflection: What burdens do you need to lay before God today?

Journal Entry:

Day 73: *Being Revived by God's Word*
Scripture: Psalm 23:1-3

Prayer: Lord, restore my soul and revive me through Your Word. Amen.

Journal Reflection: What scriptures have renewed you in the past?

Journal Entry:

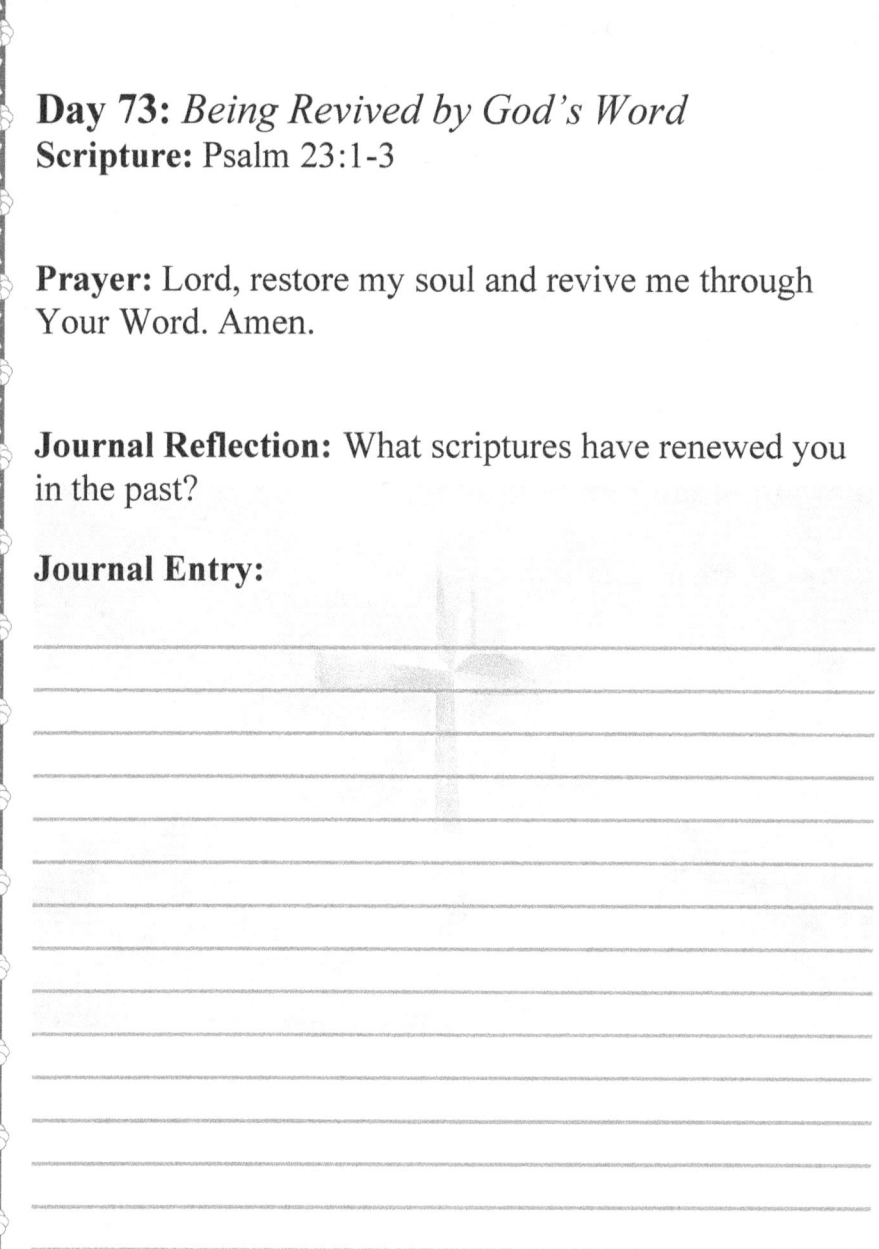

Day 74: *Trusting God for Spiritual Renewal*
Scripture: Jeremiah 17:7-8

Prayer: Father, help me trust in You as the source of my renewal. Amen.

Journal Reflection: How does trusting God help you grow spiritually?

Journal Entry:

Day 75: *The Living Water of Christ*
Scripture: John 7:37-38

Prayer: Jesus, quench my spiritual thirst with Your living water. Amen.

Journal Reflection: How can you stay spiritually refreshed each day?

Journal Entry:

Day 76: Reflection Day

Spend time journaling about what God is teaching you this week about overcoming spiritual dryness.

Journal Entry:

Day 77: Summary Day

Review the week's scriptures and journal any final thoughts on overcoming periods of spiritual dryness.

Journal Entry:

This completes **Week 11: Overcoming Spiritual Dryness.** We now turn our Attention to **Week 12: Living a Transformed Life**

Week 12: Living a Transformed Life

Theme Scripture: *Romans 12:2* – "Do not conform to the pattern of this world, but be transformed by the renewing of your mind."

Daily Entries:

Day 78: *The Power of Renewal*
Scripture: Ezekiel 11:19-20

Prayer: Lord, transform my heart and mind to reflect Your will. Amen.

Journal Reflection: What areas of your life need renewal?

Journal Entry:

Day 79: *Putting Off the Old, Putting On the New*
Scripture: Ephesians 4:22-24

Prayer: Father, help me to put off my old self and embrace the new life You offer. Amen.

Journal Reflection: What old habits or mindsets do you need to let go of?

Journal Entry:

Day 80: *Walking in the Spirit*
Scripture: Galatians 5:16-17

Prayer: Holy Spirit, guide my steps so that I may live according to Your will. Amen.

Journal Reflection: How can you be more aware of the Holy Spirit's presence in your life?

Journal Entry:

Day 81: *Transformed by the Word*
Scripture: Psalm 119:105

Prayer: Lord, let Your Word be the light that directs my steps. Amen.

Journal Reflection: How does reading God's Word change your thoughts and actions?

Journal Entry:

Day 82: *Living as a New Creation*
Scripture: 2 Corinthians 5:17

Prayer: Thank You, Lord, for making me new in Christ. Help me to walk confidently in my new identity. Amen.

Journal Reflection: What does being a "new creation" in Christ mean to you?

Journal Entry:

Day 83: Reflection Day

Spend time journaling about what God is teaching you this week on living a transformed life.

Journal Entry:

Day 84: Summary Day

Review the week's scriptures and journal any final thoughts on living a transformed life.

Journal Entry:

_____
_____
_____
_____
_____
_____
_____
_____
_____
_____
_____
_____
_____

This completes **Week 12: Living a Transformed Life** As We Come To the Conclusion our focus is **Week 13: A Thankful Heart**

Week 13: A Thankful Heart

Theme Scripture: *1 Thessalonians 5:18* – "Give thanks in all circumstances; for this is God's will for you in Christ Jesus."

Daily Entries:

Day 85: *Gratitude Opens the Heart*
Scripture: Psalm 107:1

Prayer: Lord, I give thanks to You for Your love and faithfulness. Amen.

Journal Reflection: What are five things you are thankful for today?

Journal Entry:

Day 86: *Thanking God in Every Situation*
Scripture: Philippians 4:6

Prayer: Father, help me to be grateful in all circumstances and trust in Your plan. Amen.

Journal Reflection: How can you practice gratitude even in difficult times?

Journal Entry:

Day 87: *Praising God Through Gratitude*
Scripture: Hebrews 13:15

Prayer: Lord, let my life be a continual offering of gratitude and praise to You. Amen.

Journal Reflection: How does gratitude shift your focus from problems to praise?

Journal Entry:

Day 88: *A Grateful Heart Brings Joy*
Scripture: Colossians 3:15-17

Prayer: Jesus, fill my heart with gratitude and joy that overflows to others. Amen.

Journal Reflection: How can gratitude impact your attitude and relationships?

Journal Entry:

Day 89: *Giving Thanks Always*
Scripture: Ephesians 5:20

Prayer: Lord, let me develop a habit of always giving thanks to You. Amen.

Journal Reflection: What daily practices can help you remain grateful?

Journal Entry:

Day 90: *Writing a Thank-You Note to God*
Take time to review this week's scripture and then take time to write a heartfelt note to God, expressing gratitude for His presence throughout your 90-day journey.

Journal Entry (Lord I thank you):

Final Thoughts

We pray that this **90-day journey** has set you on a new path in your walk with God. May you continue to grow in faith, deepen your trust in Him, and experience renewal, restoration, and revival in every area of your life.

We believe that this journey has already brought **victory** into your life, and we **claim it now in Jesus' name!**

To **God be the glory!** Amen.

John K Lomax
A Servant Leader

www.ingramcontent.com/pod-product-compliance
Lightning Source LLC
LaVergne TN
LVHW012247070526
838201LV00091B/148